Easy-to-Use Sermon Outline Series

SERMON OUTLINES FROM THE GOSPELS

Charles R. Wood

Grand Rapids, MI 49501

Sermon Outlines from the Gospels

Published in 1998 by Kregel Publications, a division of Kregel, Inc., P.O. Box 2607, Grand Rapids, MI 49501. Kregel Publications provides trusted, biblical publications for Christian growth and service. Your comments and suggestions are valued.

For more information about Kregel Publications, visit our web site at http://www.kregel.com

Cover and book design: Alan G. Hartman

Library of Congress Cataloging-in-Publication Data
Wood, Charles R. (Charles Robert), 1933–
Sermon outlines from the Gospels / Charles R. Wood.
p. cm. (Easy-to-use sermon outline series)
Includes index.
1. Bible. N.T. Gospels—Sermons—Outlines, syllabi, etc.
I. Title. II. Series: Wood, Charles R. (Charles Robert), 1933–
Easy-to-use sermon outline series.
BS2555.4.W66 1998 251'.02—dc21 97-42132
CIP

ISBN 0-8254-4092-0

Printed in the United States

1 2 3 / 04 03 02 01 00 99 98

Introduction

The Gospels are an incredibly fertile ground as a source of material for expository preaching. The completeness of Christ's teaching coupled with the straightforward simplicity of His style provide significant background for study, and the difficulty of interpreting some of His statements challenges thinking and stimulates exegetical activity.

The outlines that comprise this book are all derived from sermons based on passages in the Gospels. Most of the messages are drawn from passages of moderate length, although a few are based on single verses. (These "single-verse sermons," however, are usually related to a larger immediate context.)

The sermons selected for this volume were selected with two criteria particularly in view. One of those criteria was to provide a fairly broad overview of the various subjects covered in the life and ministry of the Savior. The other criteria had to do with relevance to the times in which we are preaching.

It is the opinion of the compiler of this collection that the modern church has too long been preoccupied with external matters (the sins of the "Prodigal Son") and unconcerned with internal matters (the sins of the "Prodigal Brother"). Several of these sermons deal in general with the tension between externals and internals, and many of the messages take various "sins of the spirit" as their themes.

The absence of any sermons based on passages in Mark should not be taken as significant. Many of the sermons from Matthew and Luke deal with material treated in Mark. The Matthew and Luke narratives have generally been selected because they offer a fuller treatment of the material, which is better suited to thorough exegetical work.

As is always true of books of this nature, the preacher will gain the maximum possible assistance by using this work as a stimulus and guide in preparation. Prayerful reading of the text combined with consulting one of the many single-volume commentaries available will doubtlessly produce insights undiscovered by the preacher who originally delivered these messages.

Each of the sermons outlined herein has been preached by the editor of this volume in the context of a regular, week-by-week ministry in a medium-sized local church. In most cases, the outline has been revised after it was preached to reflect lessons learned in the preaching process.

It is the prayer of the editor that the sermons contained in this book will be used of God to stimulate the preaching of others so that the glory of God will be actively promoted.

Charles R. Wood

Contents

What's in a Name?

Matthew 1:1–17

Introduction:

Some people are profoundly interested in genealogies. I find them of some interest, but hardly the stuff sermons are made of—or are they?

The genealogy of Christ is fascinating for the things it shows.

I. It Demonstrates a Cluster of Realities

A. It is structured to point to Christ

B. It shows that Christ had the proper pedigree to be the Messiah

1. It originated in Abraham (settles nationality issue)
2. It came through David (settles His right to reign)

C. In most cases the line runs through the younger brother

1. Thus the preeminence of Christ did not come through inheritance
2. Christ's greatness came as a result of the will of God

D. It may have some numerical significance

1. It is designed for memory (there are names omitted, etc.) in three groups
2. The last group is missing a name (to show God's shortening of necessary time between exile and coming of Christ?)

II. It Exposes a Group of False Assumptions

A. That Christianity is chauvinist—four women are included in the list, and with the exception of Ruth, they are not outstanding people

B. That Judaism was totally exclusive—three of the four women mentioned were foreigners, and Bathsheba would be considered one because she was married to a Hittite

C. That the Bible is a book written by human authors—until modern days, authors never made their heroes look bad, and three of the four women have blots on their characters

D. That Joseph was the father of Jesus—note the wording of verse 16

III. It Annihilates a Flock of Excuses

A. There was a strange lot in His background

1. The women already mentioned
2. At least three foreigners
3. Some rather wicked people
4. Some totally unknown individuals
5. Some good people who did terrible things

B. This mixed multitude teaches us two things
1. Individuals are not conditioned by such people in their backgrounds
2. Individuals are not influenced by what such people did

C. It speaks to the excuses of our day
1. "I can't serve the Lord because of my bad background"
2. "My mother/father was like this, so I can't help it"
3. "I don't make any difference; I'm a nobody"
4. "I have sinned so much that God could never use me"
5. "My background isn't Christian"

IV. It Advances a Series of Implications

A. The identity of Messiah

B. The source of significance—everyone finds ultimate significance in Him as He is the only source of true significance

C. The limitations of relationship—His own relatives had to receive Him! There is no salvation by ancestry, and each individual must relate to Him individually (cf. Matt. 12:46–50 with 2 Peter 3:9)

Conclusion:

There is so much in this genealogy. The two main things it shows us:

How little our genealogy actually means (His was necessary to establish His royal line), so let's get rid of all the excuses why we can't serve and obey;

How important it is to be related to the one to whom the genealogy belongs.

Righteousness, One More Time

Matthew 5:20

Introduction:

If one's righteousness must exceed that of the Pharisees to go to heaven, then the righteousness of those going to heaven ought to exceed that of the Pharisees as well.

That really isn't too big an order, given the kind of righteousness the Pharisees had.

Here are some ways in which ours ought to exceed theirs:

I. Principles Rather Than Details

A. There are generations of young people who know what to do or not do but who have no idea of why

B. This is why the Bible doesn't deal with each specific issue

II. Motives Rather Than Actions

A. The reasons why we do things are very important

1. Obedience is a good motive
2. Love out of obedience is an even better one

B. Actions are best when they arise out of proper motives

III. Being Rather Than Doing

A. What you are determines the worth of what you do

B. Constant doing without supporting that doing with being will eventually break down

IV. Reality Rather Than Appearance

A. It is important to be concerned with appearances, but things aren't always as they seem

B. The most important issue is reality—what you really are inside

V. Acceptance With God Rather Than Applause from Men

A. The Pharisees were consumed with winning men's approval

1. We tend to do what we know people will applaud
2. We avoid that which will bring disapproval

B. It is much more significant to have God's approval

VI. Relationship Rather Than Religion

A. We hesitate to call our brand of Christianity a religion

1. Religion has too much of man in it
2. Christianity is a relationship with God

B. Many are satisfied with a religion

Conclusion:

Unless there is reality, there is nothing!

Righteousness That Exceeds

Matthew 5:20

Introduction:

Just about everyone claims to have been "born again," but do we really know what it means to be such?

I. The Standard

A. The Pharisees: the most outstanding religious leaders of the time
   1. They were recognized and revered by the people
   2. They determined the course of religious life in the nation (this is why Christ tangled with them so much)
   3. They were people who claimed—appeared to have—intense righteousness

B. The basis of the righteousness of the Pharisees
   1. Religion—they were the most consistently religious people in Israel
   2. Birth—they were "Children of Abraham:" they had retained purity of breed and could trace their roots through genealogies
   3. Status—they were the most highly regarded people in the nation
   4. Performance—they kept the law with a vengeance, even to the point of growing hedges around the law
   5. Conformity—tradition was a key issue: they developed and kept it
   6. Morality—they were very moral people who were generally clear of blame

C. These are all things that people tend to depend on today

II. The Demand

A. Christ holds them up as example (He basically agrees with their outward claims)

B. He insists that one's righteousness must exceed theirs in order for one to enter heaven

C. He uses strong language to make the point perfectly clear
   1. Note key words/phrases: except, exceed, in no case
   2. There is no missing what He is saying here

III. The Dilemma

A. No one that I have ever met exceeds what is described of the Pharisees

B. Even if one could exceed them, there are other prohibitions (Gal. 2:16; Eph. 2:8–9)

C. We are called upon to exceed the Pharisees, and we are told that we can't do so

IV. The Provision

A. None of us will exceed the Pharisees
   1. Even if we do, it will not be enough
   2. Yet we are told that we must do so in order to enter the kingdom

B. When we are without hope, God provides a hope
   1. Christ was perfectly righteous—Matthew 3:15; 5:17
   2. Christ offers to give His righteousness to us

C. If we have Christ's righteousness, we have a righteousness that exceeds that of the Pharisees
   1. There might be another righteousness that exceeds it
   2. There is no other righteousness that fulfills the law

D. We can have that righteousness simply by receiving Christ—it comes with Him (1 Cor. 1:30; Rom. 10:4)

Conclusion:

Let's examine:

What makes you think you are heading for heaven? Religion? Birth? Status? Performance? Conformity? Morality?

The only righteousness that satisfies God is Christ's. Have you accepted Him and His righteousness?

A Different Spirit

Matthew 5:38–44

Introduction:

Christians are too often satisfied to be unlike the world in the way they look, but our "unlikeness" is something far deeper than that!

In fact, the teaching of Scripture is far different from the teaching of the world in which we live. Make no mistake about it.

I. The Spirit of the Christian Is to Be Different

A. Matthew 5:38–44
   1. This is one of the most radical sections in the Bible
   2. Many make the mistake of stopping with a literal interpretation
   3. We must look beyond—this describes a spirit

B. Matthew 6:19–21
   1. This also involves very radical teaching
   2. This runs totally contrary to the general spirit of our day
   3. This deals with a spirit regarding possessions, wealth, etc.

C. 1 Corinthians 6:1–8
   1. This section speaks to the whole area of litigation
   2. This philosophy is again counter to the spirit of our age
   3. The spirit involved is summarized in verse 7b

D. Romans 12:17–21
   1. Our natural tendency is to retaliate, etc.
   2. Our spirit is in view here as well—a spirit that seeks to overcome evil with good

II. The Reasons Why Our Spirit Is to Be Different

A. We are citizens of a different country—we operate under a different set of laws

B. We are products of a different culture—we have the foreigner's struggle with culture

C. We are tied to a different standard—society has various standards of conduct

D. God is our source—we can go against the world's culture because we are not dependent on it

E. We are driven by a higher motivation—our purpose is (or ought to be) to glorify God instead of what drives our society

F. We work with different priorities—we have (or should have) a different set of things that are important

G. We expect different rewards—"They have their reward" summarizes our society, but we are seeking an eternal reward

III. The Implications of Our Different Spirit

A. It changes how we think
   1. Christianity is a thinking man's religion
   2. The most common problem is that we don't think enough
   3. Christians ought to first think differently

B. It changes how we approach life
   1. Our lives have another dimension
   2. Everything ought to be filtered through the grid of our different spirit
   3. There are some important questions we always need to ask—what would the Lord have me do in this situation?

C. It changes how we act
   1. There is a specific relationship between thinking and conduct
   2. This has a very specific effect on our lives—what we do and don't do about particular situations

D. It changes how we view philosophy
   1. It should make us very leery of worldly philosophies
   2. Some specific effects:
      a. Be careful of "how to" books
      b. Be careful of counsel
      c. Be careful of "good business practice"

Conclusion:

Paul neatly summarizes in 1 Corinthians 2:12 the spirit that ought to characterize us.

One Tough Commandment

Matthew 5:44

Introduction:

Christ gave us in Scripture some tough things to do. Probably nothing we are commanded to do is any more difficult than this.

I. We Are to Do These Things For:

A. Our enemies
   1. A strong word—odious, hated, hateful
   2. This word is used to describe men at enmity against God

B. Those who curse us
   1. To curse, doom, imprecate evil on
   2. It is more than just words—it involves intentions, desires

C. Those who hate us
   1. To hate, detest
   2. To pursue with hatred—"a hatred that follows after"

D. Those who despitefully use you
   1. To insult, treat abusively, revile
   2. This is probably the most common of these negative traits

E. Those who persecute us
   1. To harass, trouble, molest
   2. This has an element of pursuit in order to do these things

II. What It Is We Are to Do for Them

A. We are to love them—strongest available word for love, which is uniformly used for love for one another

B. We are to bless them—to praise, invoke God's blessing on, ask God to bless (English word—eulogy)

C. We are to do good to them—to speak of them and do for them so that there could be no room for blame

D. We are to pray for them—to offer prayers for, speak to God about

III. Why We Should Do These Things

A. Because God commands them
   1. This really settles it
   2. We could stop here, but Christ doesn't

B. Because doing so recognizes God's sovereignty (v. 45)

1. He exercises His right to do as He pleases
2. He has chosen to treat all alike—we confirm His right to that when we do so also

C. Because doing so conforms to the mind of Christ
   1. We are to have His mind (Phil. 2:8)
   2. We have His example (Luke 23:34; 1 Pet. 2:21–23)

D. Because doing so shows something to the unsaved (v. 46–47)
   1. It shows something different from what they are accustomed to
   2. It shows something more than they are capable of

E. Because doing so is good for us
   1. It tries and proves our obedience
   2. It gives God opportunity to work on our behalf
   3. It forces us to examine our motives, etc.

F. Because doing so is a mark of maturity (v. 48)
   1. This kind of living takes spiritual maturity
   2. The more we do this, the more we replicate Christ

Conclusion:

The difficulty of a commandment has no bearing on our responsibility to keep that commandment. This is especially true in light of the indwelling presence of the Holy Spirit, who is designed to assist our obedience. This is one tough commandment, but we have no excuse for not keeping it.

A Perfect Pattern for Prayer

Matthew 6:9–13

Introduction:

This really isn't the Lord's prayer. That is in John 17. This is actually the disciples' prayer. There is no real problem with its repetition, but it doesn't appear it was ever intended to be repeated "as is."

The actual introduction reads: "This, then, is how you should pray. . ."

I. Premises

A. This is a matter of relationship
   1. None but the child of God can pray this
   2. It stresses that we are in a family relationship with Him

B. This is a matter of reverence
   1. It marks off the difference and distance between us
   2. It sounds a caution about over-familiarity

II. Principles

A. Stated
   1. Concern for God's name—the name stands for the person and for the person's honor
   2. Concern for God's rule—the rule and reign of Christ and its growth in human hearts and its establishment on earth
   3. Concern for God's will—perfectly obeyed in heaven, it calls for such obedience on earth

B. Applied
   1. It should condition all our prayer and rule out some prayer
   2. It explains what appears to be unanswered prayer
   3. It explains unrelieved suffering (Paul's thorn in the flesh)

III. Petitions

A. For needs
   1. This is a daily matter—"day by day" bread (our need for each day)
   2. Involves: moderation, trust, dependence, humility, generosity

B. For forgiveness
   1. This is critical—we are forgiven in salvation, but we must be forgiven as we go through life

2. This is conditional—this is difficult to understand, but it appears certain that many prayers are hindered because of unforgiveness and bitterness

C. For spiritual victory

1. Over things we can't help—things that just happen along the course of life
2. Over things we experience—things that come from "the evil one"

IV. Perspective

A. You possess the rule

1. The kingdom is already yours
2. There is no question of who is in charge

B. You possess the power

1. Everything that is asked is within your ability
2. This stresses the point of prayer

C. You possess the glory

1. That is the "end view" item in the prayer
2. This brings the prayer back to its beginning

Conclusion:

Notice some things about this prayer:

Its brevity, its focus on God, its coverage of various areas: human need, human relationships, human spiritual development. This should teach us some things about prayer. What is your underlying purpose in prayer? Are you meeting the requirement regarding forgiveness? Are you achieving in prayer?

As James says: ". . . ye have not, because ye ask not. Ye ask, and receive not, because ye ask amiss."

Wholehearted

Matthew 6:33

Introduction:

We need a life-purpose and a statement of it. Let's see if we can find something general for everyone. Here is a general statement of purpose.

I. The Statement Exists in a Context (vv. 25–34)

- A. It deals with worry over temporal needs
- B. It shows that:
  1. Such worry is pointless
  2. Such worry is unnecessary
  3. Such worry is sinful
- C. "If you want to worry, I'll give you something to worry about; namely, your relationship to the Father."

II. The Statement Involves a Contrast (v. 32)

- A. These are things the Gentiles (heathen) around you worry about
- B. You are different from them
  1. They are outside the kingdom
  2. They have no promise of His provision
  3. This is an area in which the difference can show
- C. Some of the heathen are smarter than God's children—they don't worry

III. The Statement Demands a Commitment (v. 33)

- A. Seek: strong word
  1. Be absorbed in the search for, a persevering, strenuous effort
  2. Be continually seeking
- B. Kingdom/righteousness
  1. Kingdom: the place where Christ rules and reigns
  2. Righteousness: His righteous character
  3. Advance His kingdom: know Him better, be more like Him
- C. First
  1. In priority (importance)
  2. In time (early)
  3. In preference (choices)
- D. A sample statement of purpose: to put first priority in life on advancing His realm on earth, knowing Him better, and being more like Him

IV. The Statement Promises a Contribution

A. This is a cause and effect statement: "If you . . ., then I . . ."
   1. If you continuously seek His kingdom/righteousness first
   2. Then the things in view in the passage will be added to you

B. We talk about giving to God; actually, God gives to us

C. This speaks of a worry-free supply based on prioritized living

V. The Statement Presents a Challenge

A. How are you seeking to advance His kingdom on earth?

B. How are you seeking to know Him better and to be more like Him?

C. When is the last time you consciously went without something in the interest of His kingdom?

D. When (and how) did you last put the interests of His kingdom ahead of other interests in life?

Conclusion:

One last question: How are you going to live out the implications of this verse? Your answer will pretty much express your life purpose.

Definitive Doing

Matthew 7:15–29

Introduction:

There are two significant documents in connection with Christ: The Sermon on Mount—a definitive statement at the beginning of His ministry; The Lord's Prayer in John 17—a definitive statement at the close of His ministry. The last three sections of the Sermon on the Mount deal with the same theme—getting the Bible into life. "Doing the will of God" involves being what the Bible says I should be and doing what the Bible says I should do.

I. A Point of Discrimination (vv. 15–20): "Ye shall know them by their fruits" (vv. 16, 20 KJV)

- A. Caution (v. 15)
  1. Watch out for false prophets
  2. They look (try to look) like sheep, but actually they are ferocious wolves (that seek to devour)
- B. Criteria (vv. 16–18)—lessons from nature
  1. Trees bear the same kind of fruit as the tree itself—good and bad trees can't bear opposite fruit
  2. Good trees bear good fruit; bad trees bear bad fruit
- C. Condemnation (v. 19)
  1. Bad trees are ultimately hewn down
  2. Bad trees are subject to judgment

II. A Principle of Distinction (vv. 21–23)

- A. Claims (v. 22)
  1. We have prophesied
  2. We have cast out demons
  3. We have done many wonderful works
- B. Conduct
  1. We have done good things
  2. We have done them in the name of the Lord
  3. We have done them over a long period of time
- C. Consequences (v. 23)
  1. "I never knew you"
  2. "Depart from me"
  3. The issue—"he that doeth the will of my Father" (the one involved in doing what God wants done)

III. A Parable of Determination (vv. 24–27)

- A. Contractors

    1. Two men here
    2. May know their names (Rocky and Sandy)
B. Construction
    1. Two houses were built
    2. The houses may have been identical, but the foundations were radically different
C. Crisis
    1. The storm is the same—extremely severe
    2. The storm represents the storms of life or judgment
D. Conclusion
    1. The house on the rock stood—because on the rock
    2. The house on the sand fell—because not on the rock
    3. The rock—doing the will of God ("Everyone who hears these words of mine and puts them into practice")

Conclusion:

Three questions answered: 1) How to tell a true teacher; 2) How to tell a true conversion; 3) How to tell a true Christian.

Two cautions issued: 1) People are not necessarily what they claim to be; 2) People are not necessarily what they appear to be.

One message communicated: THE KEY TO DIFFERENTIATION is the way a life lines up by the Word of God.

Little Faith and Great Faith

Matthew 8:5–13; Matthew 15:21–28

Introduction:

"You can get anything you want from God if you have enough faith." The opposite of this is the idea that when you wanted something and didn't get it, you didn't have enough faith. "If we only had great faith—reserved for a certain few—we could really see things happen." Christ did commend great faith and condemn little faith, but there's more to the story.

I. **Basic Truth**
   A. Can we really "get anything we want from God"?
   B. Two passages appear to indicate that we can (Matt. 17:20; Luke 17:6)
   C. Actually, however, they teach how little faith is necessary to achieve
      1. The emphasis is on the amount necessary for great things
      2. Both statements are in the form of a rebuke
      3. They don't really teach what is claimed

II. **The Demonstration of Great Faith**
   A. It is not something all that special
      1. The two commended for it were both non-Jews
      2. Neither was anything special spiritually
   B. What's notable about the centurion?
      1. He recognized Christ's authority
      2. He recognized Christ's ability
   C. What's notable about the woman?
      1. She persevered—would not take "no" for an answer
      2. She banked on His willingness
   D. What's notable about the two together
      1. Both asked for something He was obviously doing
      2. Both thus showed a commitment to the will of God

III. **The Nature of Great Faith**
   A. Faith is operating on fact
      1. Both people went on the facts they had
      2. The greater the commitment to act on fact, the greater the faith
   B. Confirmed by people condemned for little faith
      1. Matthew 8:26
      2. Matthew 14:31
      3. Matthew 16:8

IV. The Contents of Great Faith

A. It recognizes who God is
B. It accepts His absolute authority
C. It accepts His complete ability
D. It persists in its mission
E. It stays serious about what it desires
F. It is totally committed to the will of God

Conclusion:

Surely more can be accomplished than we see, and more accomplished than others do. It is just a matter of accepting the facts and acting on them.

Through His Eyes

Matthew 9:35–10:1

Introduction:

I often wish others could see things through my eyes, but I don't do too well at seeing through the eyes of others. We all need to do so. What we really need to do, however, is to see things through the eyes of Christ.

I. He Saw Needs (v. 35)

A. He saw their needs and how He could meet them; we see our needs and how they can meet them

B. We are cool toward evangelism and weak toward missions because we don't see needs

1. We aren't out where needs are (He was)
2. We often aren't looking

C. We likely miss many opportunities to minister/evangelize because we are not out there looking for them

II. He Saw Reality (v. 36)

A. He saw people for what they were

1. "Fainted"—shorn (fleeced) and left weak
2. "Scattered abroad"—thrown down
3. Shepherdless—without care, oversight, leadership (those that should have helped were adding to the problems)

B. We see people for what they appear to be: satisfied, smug, successful, secure, etc.

C. People are no different today than they were then

1. They are still characterized by the same facts
2. They are still being sold out by those who should help

III. He Saw Potential (v. 37)

A. "The harvest"—that which may be reaped, i.e., people

B. "Is plenteous" (KJV)—there is much (are many) to be harvested (this certainly doesn't seem to be so)

C. "The laborers are few"

1. This expresses the limitation; the problem is lack of laborers
2. This explains the situation on the mission field and homeland as well

IV. He Saw Resources (v. 38)

A. "Pray"—don't grow bitter, try to manipulate, etc.
B. "The Lord of the harvest"—He controls the harvest
C. "That He will send"
D. "Laborers"—here is part of the problem, there is some work involved
   1. The quality is more important than the quantity
   2. He knows who best can do the work
E. "Into HIS harvest"—it is His harvest, not ours!

V. He Saw Responsibility (10:1–5)

A. Note the process
   1. He told the disciples to pray
   2. He called them to Him
   3. He sent them forth to do the job
B. The principle here—the laborers come from among the disciples
C. The more we walk with Him, the more likely we are to reap in the harvest

Conclusion:

Seeing things through the eyes of Christ . . .
Will change our view of missions;
Will change our view of evangelism;
Will change our view of Christian ministry.

Father, Forgive Them

Matthew 18:15–35

Introduction:

We think in categories and outlines, whereas Christ taught in stories, metaphors, and similarities. This passage is a case in point.

I. The Drama of Forgiveness
- A. Christ provides clear instructions (vv. 15–20)
- B. Christ makes a radical statement (vv. 21–22)
- C. Christ tells a graphic story (vv. 23–35)

II. The Demands of Forgiveness
- A. The proper way to handle offenses
- B. The correct approach to handling confessions ("I was wrong")
- C. The biblical attitude toward forgiveness—grant it when requested; give it when it is not

III. The Dynamics of Forgiveness—Failure to Forgive:
- A. Creates a role reversal
  1. Note in the story that the servant becomes a master
  2. God's role is to call others into account
- B. Indicates a lack of Christlikeness
  1. He said, "Father, forgive them . . ."
  2. Note 1 Peter 2:21–25
- C. Shows deep disobedience
  1. We are commanded to forgive—by His teaching
  2. To fail to forgive is to fail to obey
- D. Makes our problem obvious to others
  1. An unforgiving spirit rarely stands alone
  2. It always shows, and we look worse than the person we won't forgive
- E. Blocks us from finding forgiveness ourselves
  1. Very clear that 1 John 1:9 is conditioned
  2. Cf. Matthew 6:12–15; Mark 11:25–26
- F. Leads to bitterness
  1. Unforgiveness seldom stands alone
  2. Bitterness is usually the reason for unforgiveness
- G. Grieves the Holy Spirit
  1. It hinders our prayers as well as our forgiveness
  2. Note Ephesians 4:30–32

H. Blights other lives that we touch
   1. Hebrews 12:15
   2. Bitterness affects and infects others
I. Makes us subject to punishment
   1. Note verses 34–35
   2. This may be another graphic, vivid statement designed to draw attention—it must involve a very serious consequence
J. Demonstrates lack of confidence in God
   1. Notice what He has said: "Vengeance is mine; I will repay, saith the Lord" (Rom. 12:19 KJV)
   2. Don't worry about the other person getting away with anything—God will take care of it

IV. The Direction of Forgiveness

A. We should be characterized by a forgiving spirit
   1. He is driving for more than just the specific instances here
   2. We never will show Christlikeness until we have such a spirit
B. Forgiveness is a matter of the mind and will
   1. We forgive in the mind, in our thinking
   2. We choose to forgive by an act of the will (can't say "I can't" or any other cliché; must say "I won't")

Conclusion:

Christ said that offenses will come. We must forgive them, face the offender with the offense or put ourselves in jeopardy. "If ye forgive not, neither will your Father . . . forgive your trespasses."

A Strange, Soul-Searching Story

Matthew 20:1–16

Introduction:

Most parables are fairly simple to interpret and straightforward to apply. There are two exceptions to this, and this story is one of them. Here's a strange story, difficult to interpret but soul-searching.

I. The Strange Story

A. Day laborer concept
   1. This is somewhat uncommon today
   2. This was routine and regular then

B. Several groups were hired
   1. The first and last groups are most important
   2. We have little detail on the others

C. A time of reckoning
   1. The owner took groups in reverse order deliberately
   2. He forced the first group to see what the last group got

D. Remuneration
   1. The last group got what the first group was promised
   2. The first group got what it was promised

E. Remonstrance
   1. The first group was incensed by its treatment
   2. They got their reward, but they effectually lost it

II. The Interpretation of the Story

A. Proper interpretation—go back and pick up the context
   1. The story of rich young ruler
   2. This precipitated Peter's question
   3. This parable is designed to answer errors in Peter's question

B. The errors of Peter
   1. "This man went away; we didn't. Aren't we the good guys?"—this is a matter of pride
   2. "This man went away; we didn't. What's in it for us?"—this demonstrates serving the Lord with a mercenary spirit
   3. "This man went away. He doesn't deserve anything."—this demonstrates a tendency to look at others, etc.

C. The correction of the errors
   1. The ones who were there all day lose much through a bad spirit
   2. The ones who served all day got what was agreed upon
   3. The ones who served actually "lost their reward" in their concern with what others got (actually envy here)

III. The Soul-Searching of the Story—Beware of:

A. Pride
   1. It isn't how lucky He is that we serve—it is how incredible that He would allow us to serve
   2. Pride always makes us think we are better than we are

B. A mercenary spirit
   1. Danger: don't serve with a "what's in it for me?" spirit
   2. They got what was agreed upon
   3. We get what was agreed upon—eternal life, indwelling Spirit, supply of need, tribulation, persecution, etc.

C. Invidious comparisons
   1. What anyone else gets is really none of your business
   2. What anyone else does is also none of your business
   3. We need to look to ourselves and our relationship with the Lord

Conclusion:

Peter watched the exchange with the rich young ruler, reflected on that exchange, and drew some wrong conclusions. Christ corrected Peter and gave us information. The basic teaching of the parable?

Watch your attitude in serving the Lord.

Don't pride yourself on being better than others. The very presence of pride sullies our character.

Don't get caught in a mercenary spirit.

Don't worry about what God does with or for others. Looking at others will usually make us proud or dissatisfied.

The Sin of Unbelief

Luke 1:5–25

Introduction:

The story of Zacharias is a "Christmas Prelude," but it is a prelude played on an instrument that is out of tune. Unfortunately, Zacharias speaks to us too pertinently for comfort.

I. A Portrait of Zacharias

A. Old Testament prophesy spoke of one who would come before Messiah—this is that story

B. Details

1. An older priest with a barren wife
2. He had repeatedly sought the Lord's favor on her barrenness
3. He comes to Jerusalem to fulfill priestly functions
4. He is in the process of doing so when he is accosted by an angel
5. The angel promises him the child for which he has prayed
6. He reacts with a measure of disbelief
7. He is given the sign of inability to speak (was he deaf as well?—see verse 62)

II. The Problem of Zacharias

A. His basic problem—unbelief

B. Unbelief in the face of reasons to believe

1. He was a believer—faithful in Israel
2. He had been instructed/was enlightened (a teacher of others); he knew that God had done this very thing before
3. He was a leader and supposed to be an example, but he stumbled at what others had believed
4. He was given a clear message (an angel, in the temple, while praying, etc.)
5. He had been praying for the very thing that he was promised

C. Our unbelief is equally blameworthy

1. We have the record of the Word of God (the assurance of its promises is even more sure than angelic appearance)
2. We have the memory of previous favors from God

III. The Punishment of Zacharias

A. Remember that it was for unbelief

B. What it involved

1. Humiliation—he was made to look foolish
2. Debilitation—it was incredibly disabling
3. Correction—it kept him from expressing further unbelief
4. Beneficial—it forced him to thoughtful reflection

C. We may not be punished for unbelief, but there is always some loss incurred

IV. The Pointers from Zacharias

A. Man's unbelief does not invalidate God's promises/purposes/plans

1. God did what He was going to do, only Zacharias did not have the full enjoyment of it
2. God always does what He is planning to do

B. Caution—some of God's promises/purposes/plans are conditional on belief

1. Many promises of provision have an "if" attached
2. We don't thwart God's plan, but we do hinder our own reception of it

C. Beware of a focus on the difficulty of God's promises/purposes/plans

1. Zacharias's problem was the difficulty of the thing promised
2. We need a reminder that nothing is impossible with God

D. The ultimate curse of unbelief is failing to believe what God has said about sin, salvation, and eternal life

Conclusion:

We don't think of unbelief as sin, but it is. It was serious enough to result in punishment for Zacharias. It is serious enough to condemn men to hell. Are you guilty? What will you do about it?

Why Bother?

Luke 5:1–11

Introduction:

Do you ever get frustrated? You do something that seems to have no results whatever. You begin to wonder, "Why bother?"

I. The Problems That Plague Us

A. You take a stand in your world, and it has no effect
B. You seek to win others to Christ and have no success
C. You pray for an unsaved or wayward loved one, but there is no change
D. You spend a lot of time and effort seeking to help someone who peters out or turns against you
E. You do good to someone, and there is no return
F. You minister faithfully, but it appears there are no results
G. You strive to keep a testimony before an unsaved mate who only grows more difficult as time goes by
H. You begin to wonder—Why bother?

II. The Example That Enlightens Us

A. Peter (and others) were doing what they knew to do
B. They had fished all night without results
C. Christ now tells them to fish where they know there are no fish
D. Peter expresses it: Why bother?
E. Peter's next words explain it all—"Nevertheless at thy word" (v. 5 KJV)
F. Peter does the pointless because Christ told him to do it

III. The Consequences That Challenge Us

A. The disciples received a supernatural return
  1. It came after a long time of action
  2. It goes along with Galatians 6:9
B. Sometimes the repayment is postponed
  1. 1 Corinthians 4:5
  2. When the motivations of hearts are revealed, each will receive praise from God
C. Even if there is never a reward, there will be praise from Him because we have done what was right because it was right

Conclusion:

Why bother? Because He said so! There will either be a harvest—possibly after a long time—or there will be praise in eternity.

Eliminate the Weeds

Luke 8:4–15 (esp. 14)

Introduction:

There are 205 varieties of weeds in America, and it is likely you have two-thirds of them in your yard. But there are also weeds in our personal lives, and weeds are deadly to being a productive person. To be productive, we need to get after the weeds.

I. The Identification of Weeds

A. The cares of this world
   1. This has to do with the things that worry us (Matt. 6:25–34)
   2. Everyday life has enough cares to keep us unproductive

B. Riches
   1. Most don't need to worry about this?—quite the contrary
   2. This has to do with the pursuit of money (Matt. 6:19–21)
   3. The process of securing our finances can keep us unproductive (so many have time to pursue spiritual realities)

C. The pleasures of this world
   1. The pursuit of leisure
   2. This has become a major preoccupation of our society

II. The Nature of Weeds

A. They grow on their own
   1. There is no need to cultivate them
   2. They grow best when we are unaware of them

B. They choke out the good stuff
   1. This is why it is necessary to weed the garden
   2. They rob us of time, energy, and money

C. They give an appearance of life
   1. They are normally green, profuse, etc. (we have to get close to them to see what they really are)
   2. They are of little value

III. The Treatment of Weeds

A. Recognize the weeds
   1. It is sometimes difficult to tell the difference
   2. We can't root out what we don't know exists

B. Reject the weeds
   1. We need a determination of will not to be filled with weeds
   2. We probably will never get them completely out; we will have to come back and work on them again

C. Resist the weeds
   1. Get a biblical perspective on what constitutes a weed
   2. Try to keep them from taking root in your life

Conclusion:

For your garden—even trees—to produce, you must get rid of the weeds. For you to be a productive person, you must deal with the weeds in life: the cares of life, money, and leisure. What changes need to be made? What are you going to do about it?

Which One Will Love Most?

Luke 7:36–50

Introduction:

Christ deals here with the great theme of forgiveness. The question regarding forgiveness involves how it is secured. Some believe it comes in response to contrition, and they appear to take their direction from this passage. But something else is in view here.

I. The Incident That Prompted the Parable (vv. 36–40)

A. An invitation
   1. He was invited by a Pharisee
   2. He accepted it as He always went to needy people

B. An invasion
   1. It was not strange for someone to enter the house
   2. It was strange for a woman to do so
   3. It was even stranger for this woman to enter the house of a Pharisee
   4. Her approach to the table and her action were even stranger

C. Incredulity
   1. Note the Pharisee's thoughts
   2. His logic and reasoning were impeccable

D. Insight
   1. Christ read his mind
   2. Christ answered him through this parable

II. The Parable That Rebuked the Pharisee (vv. 41–42)

A. The story: creditor; two debtors; two debts; both forgiven

B. The question: Which one will love him the most?

C. The answer: The one who is forgiven the most

D. The response: Your answer is correct

III. The Teaching That Applied the Parable (vv. 43–50)

A. The contrast
   1. "Look at this woman"
   2. She did all the things you should have done and didn't do

B. The conclusion
   1. Her sins are already forgiven
   2. This is shown by the fact that she loves much
   3. Those who love little show little forgiveness

C. The challenge
    1. He declares what she has already experienced
    2. He declares how she was saved
    3. He dismisses her in peace

IV. The Applications That Enliven the Parable

A. The source of forgiveness
    1. Was she forgiven by contrition?
    2. No! She was forgiven as a result of faith

B. The demonstrations of forgiveness—action

C. The product of forgiveness—gratitude

D. The effect of forgiveness—"go in peace" (assurance and peace)

Conclusion:

Was this woman forgiven because she was contrite, or was she grateful because she was forgiven? She was grateful because she was forgiven. She had already been forgiven—to see it any other way misses the whole point of the story.

The Samaritan We Call Good

Luke 10:25–37

Introduction:

As often, this parable is part of a larger picture. We need to see the whole to understand this part.

I. The Provocation

A. The initial question (v. 25)
   1. The desire to "put him to the test"
   2. This was a common question among religious Jews

B. The answering question (v. 26)
   1. This was a common method of Christ
   2. "You are an expert on the law—what do you think?"

C. The further response (v. 27)
   1. This is a summary of the two tables of the law
   2. This is a common answer of the time

D. The commendation (v. 28)
   1. Christ completely agreed with him (Matt. 22:37–39; Mark 12:28–31)
   2. Mark Christ's answer well

E. The further question (v. 29)
   1. There was general agreement on the answer; multiplied questions on the meaning of the answer
   2. Wanting to make himself qualify, he focused on the second area

II. The Parable

A. Christ told this story to answer the question about "neighborness" (vv. 30–35)
   1. The details of the man's problem (v. 30)
   2. The details of those passing by (vv. 31–32)
   3. The details of the Samaritan's actions (vv. 33–35)

B. Christ asked him a question about the story (v. 36)
   1. In the process, He turned the question around: from "Who is my neighbor?" to "To whom am I neighbor?"
   2. He took the issue from passive to active status

C. Christ told him to go and do the same (v. 37)
   1. Note the repetition of words in verse 28
   2. He told him to follow the pattern provided

III. The Principles

A. The danger of self-vindication
   1. The lawyer considered himself a keeper of the law
   2. When we pride ourselves on some spiritual achievement, we usually are blind to some area of the matter

B. The issue of salvation by good works
   1. The standard has been presented
   2. Our inability has been demonstrated
   3. God's righteousness has been vindicated—Christ has perfectly kept the law, and we have kept the law in Him

C. The matter of "neighbor"
   1. The answer to the proper question, "To whom am I neighbor?" I am neighbor to anyone in need, anytime I am capable of helping
   2. The extent of my "neighborness"
      a. To my enemies (Golden Rule operates here) (Luke 6:32–5)
      b. To my brethren (1 John 3:16–18)
      c. To all men (Gal. 6:9–10)
   3. The necessity for action—there is more required than just recognizing the situation; I must take any action within my ability (James 2:14–16)

Conclusion:

We don't get saved by keeping the law. We don't get standing by keeping the law. We have standing in Christ. Because we have standing, we are obligated to love our neighbor, who is anyone in need, anytime we are able to help.

The Hardest Words in the Whole Wide World

Luke 15:18

Introduction:

There are two things Christians are terrible at: accepting rebuke and admitting to wrong. "I was wrong" may be the most underused phrase.

I. Cases

A. Saul (1 Sam. 12:8–12; 15:12–15; 24:16–22)
   1. He was twice confronted regarding major disobedience
   2. He twice blames the people rather than saying, "I was wrong"
   3. When he does admit to wrong, it is done obliquely

B. David (2 Sam. 11–12; Pss. 32, 51)
   1. David sinned with Bathsheba
   2. He went through a time of tremendous turmoil
   3. He only said "I was wrong" after a direct confrontation from God

C. The Prodigal (Luke 15)
   1. He acted in self-will
   2. He got into a terrible mess
   3. He only said "I was wrong" after there was nowhere else to turn (a bit better than David, but not too good)

D. Daniel (9:3ff.)
   1. We have nothing of negative nature recorded about him
   2. Yet he prays a phenomenal prayer—he identifies himself with the sin of his people even though he has not sinned
   3. He found it very easy to say "I was wrong"

II. Causes

A. Suggested ones:
   1. Inadequacy
   2. Insecurity
   3. Immaturity
   4. Pride/arrogance (some people will admit wrong in the abstract, but never in the specific)

B. Illustrated
   1. Saul—inadequate (insecure?)
   2. David—proud

3. The Prodigal—immature

III. The Curse

A. It makes a person look like a fool
B. It causes problems for self and for others
C. It impedes development of spiritual graces
D. It renders one unable to deal with problems in a biblical manner
E. It assures that one can't be granted forgiveness
F. It makes it more difficult to face and deal with sin
G. It hardens the heart against conviction—makes us cold and indifferent

IV. The Cure

A. Gain a sense of perspective
   1. Be sure your God is big enough
   2. Be sure you see yourself for what you really are
B. Pray for God to show you where you are wrong
C. Resolve to admit wrong where God shows it
D. Approach admission of wrong in a biblical manner
   1. Forget apologies
   2. Wrong demands forgiveness
   3. The correct statement is "I was wrong; will you forgive me?"

Conclusion:

The hardest words in the whole wide world are "I was wrong." When is the last time you said, "I was wrong. Will you forgive me?"?

Two Pairs

Luke 15:25–32; 18:9–14

Introduction:

There is much for us to learn from these two stories—much about self-righteousness.

Technical: self-righteousness is the idea that there is righteousness in self.

Practical: self-righteousness is viewing one's self as more righteous than others.

The signs of self-righteousness:

I. Complacency

A. The content of complacency:
   1. Self-satisfaction—a sense of having arrived, of not needing much else
   2. Self-congratulation—sending oneself messages, a matter of excessive self-concept
   3. Self-promotion—pushing oneself as the standard or promoting one's own agenda
   4. Self-expression—one who is usually very free in expressing his own position, etc.

B. The contrasts to complacency
   1. 1 Timothy 2:12–15
   2. 1 Corinthians 15:9
   3. Ephesians 3:8
   4. Mark 9:35; 10:44
   5. Philippians 3:13

II. Comparison

A. The criteria of comparison
   1. My righteousness: "I am right and righteous, and I get to define righteousness"
   2. My practice: "The way I do it is right, and no one else's way of doing things is right"
   3. My interpretation: "I alone understand Scripture, and I determine what is binding for everyone"
   4. My superiority: "I am better than others (in practice if not in thought)"

B. The condemnation of comparison
   1. Matthew 7:1
   2. Luke 6:37
   3. John 7:24
   4. 1 Corinthians 4:3–5

5. Romans 14:3–4, 10–13

III. Criticism

A. The character of criticism—everybody and everything
   1. He criticized his brother
   2. He criticized his father—you can't criticize your brother without criticizing your father
   3. He criticized the merriment and party
   4. He criticized honoring his brother—he was probably not happy his brother had returned

B. The correction of criticism
   1. Numbers 11:1
   2. Philippians 2:14
   3. 1 Corinthians 10:6–10
   4. Proverbs 13:10
   5. Ephesians 4:31

Conclusion:

Self-righteousness is very common. It is a result of our natural problem with pride, and it appears to be a tool of Satan as well. When we become complacent and begin to compare ourselves with others and begin to criticize everyone and everything, we stop being biblical. Remember ". . . he that humbleth himself shall be exalted" (v. 14 KJV).

Must We Believe in Hell?

Luke 16:19–31

Introduction:

Unbelievers deny its existence, and uninformed believers doubt it. It has been called cruel, inhumane, and barbarous, and it seems too harsh a punishment just for failing to believe. But the issue of hell stands ever before us. Must we believe in hell? Yes! In a day when many are changing basic beliefs, we still believe in a real, literal hell for the following reasons:

I. The Bible Teaches It

A. Jesus taught it
   1. This story—it is probably not a parable because of the specific name used
   2. There are other references (Matt. 10:28; Matt. 25:41; Mark 9:43–44)

B. The greater N.T. teaches it
   1. Revelation 20:13–15
   2. 2 Thessalonians 1:7–9

II. God's Love Demands It

A. Love is often used as argument against it; it is actually an argument for it

B. Love cannot act coercively, only persuasively (He cannot ravish; He can only woo—because He is loving); thus love demands:
   1. Those who do not wish to love Him must be allowed not to love Him
   2. Those who do not wish to be with Him must be allowed separation

III. Human Dignity Requires It

A. Forcing people to do something against their wills affronts their dignity

B. There are two kinds of people: those who say to God, "Thy will be done" and those to whom God says "Thy will be done"

C. Forcing people to go to heaven against their will would turn heaven into hell for them

D. The very people who fight against hell are those who insist on freedom of the human will (you can't have it both ways)

IV. God's Justice Insists on It

A. Justice demands a reward for good and punishment for evil

B. God has chosen not to finalize judgment in this life (this is the reason why it is correct to say that life isn't fair)

C. There must be a place of reward for goodness and punishment for evil in the future or life makes no sense

V. God's Sovereignty Determines It

A. The Bible speaks of God's sovereignty some day being absolute

B. Sovereignty is not finally absolute unless good triumphs over evil

C. The triumph of good over evil is not meaningful without separation

VI. The Cross Presupposes It

A. The Cross is at the center of Christianity

B. The Cross is the means of salvation

C. Jesus endured great suffering on the cross

D. Why the Cross if there is no hell?

1. No hell to shun? The Cross a sham!
2. There is no significance to the Cross if there is no eternal separation from God

Conclusion:

Two towering questions:

Do you believe in hell?

If you do, have you done anything about it?

Better to prepare to avoid hell and find it doesn't exist than to find it does exist when you are not prepared to avoid it.

Lessons from Some Lepers

Luke 17:11–19

Introduction:

This is an interesting little story told only by Luke. For such a simple story, it is filled with significance. There are at least ten lessons we can draw from these lepers:

I. The Essential of Faith

A. They had faith enough to seek Him and to do what He said to do; dominated by doubt, they would have died lepers

B. Nothing meaningful ever happens spiritually without faith

II. The Importance of Obedience

A. Those who expect Christ's favors must obey His commands

B. Had they not done what He said—or demanded something more dramatic, etc.—they would have missed healing

C. Disobedient saints miss so much of God's blessings!

III. The General Ingratitude of Mankind

A. Faith enough to be healed is not always faith enough to be grateful

B. How often we hear requests; how seldom we hear praise

IV. The Commitment to Doing Good

A. He did for them in spite of knowing they would be ungrateful

B. This is the meaning of "right is its own reward"

C. Doing good should be based on need, not on potential response

V. The Grace of God in Christ

A. In spite of their lack of gratitude, they kept the blessing

B. Human ingratitude is not answered by divine retraction

C. Fortunately, lack of gratitude does not sacrifice most blessings

VI. The Rebuke of the Samaritan

A. The grateful man was a hated Samaritan

B. Those we look down upon often excel us in virtue

VII. **The Superiority of Spiritual Relationship**

A. We assume he came back to Christ before visiting the priests; the others just went their way through a religious routine

B. Many are more concerned with (religious) routine than with any real relationship—we see this around us every day

VIII. **The Urgency of Praise**

A. The one who came back got something more

B. Failure of praise resulted in eternal loss for the others

C. We likely lose blessings when we fail to praise

IX. **The Benefits of Gratitude**

A. Nine were healed; one was saved

B. This is because only one bothered to show gratitude

X. **The Uniqueness of Christ**

A. They called out to Him

B. They knew He was the only place to go for help

C. You will ultimately find help in no other place than in Christ

D. Leprosy then was incurable; it could only be healed

E. Sin is incurable; it can only be forgiven

Conclusion:

We set our blessings under a bushel and our needs on a hillside. In which group would you find yourself?

How's Business?

Luke 19:11–28

Introduction:

The Lord understood business—there are sound management principles in His teaching. He used business examples in several instances. The identifications are easy: Lord—Jesus; servants—Christians; enemies—unsaved society; pounds—things pertaining to His kingdom.

I. The Master's Donation

A. He gave them each something
   1. Everyone received the same thing
   2. Everyone received the same amount
   3. The amount was not huge but significant (one-third of a year's pay)
   4. Everyone received whether or not he wanted to
   5. Everyone was required to do business: "occupy" (KJV) means to transact business

B. It was left to them
   1. To decide where to use it
   2. To decide how best to use it
   3. To use their own judgment in the situation

II. The Master's Departure

A. He went seeking the kingdom

B. The result of His departure
   1. He left them among his enemies
   2. They were neither to hoard nor waste the master's goods

C. The certainty of his return

III. The Master's Demand

A. The accounting
   1. Note the first man's words—"thy pound"
   2. Note the difference between five and ten—the key issue, however, is one of faithfulness
   3. The reward is proportional to faithfulness "in a very little [thing]"

B. He had no desire to gain from them
   1. He was not making money but building character
   2. He desired not to gain from them but to educate them

C. He said, "well done"—splendid!

IV. The Master's Declaration

A. Note his exchange with the unprofitable servant
   1. "I didn't do anything"
   2. He still had the pound (he couldn't unload his responsibility)

B. "Take from the one who has not and give to the one that has"
   1. It doesn't involve losing salvation but rather benefits, etc.
   2. "Use it or lose it" is entirely biblical ("The one who grows rich through diligence will grow richer; the one who has grown poor through slothfulness will grow poorer" [Morgan].)

V. The Master's Design

A. Verse 11 implies kingdom expectations; He was showing:
   1. The kingdom would not come at once
   2. The character of the kingdom would be more of commerce than of the military

B. The specific purposes of the donation?
   1. To put servants to the test
   2. To develop them
   3. To prepare them for the future
   4. To give them opportunity to achieve
   5. To provide the motivation of anticipation

Conclusion:

"With the pound they must do business." The question is not whether or not we want to do it, but how we are doing at it!

"Everyone is responsible for the prosecution of the commerce of heaven in the interest of the absent king. Until He comes again, it is our business to prosecute His enterprize in the world."

How's business?

Free Indeed

John 8:31–36

Introduction:

Freedom has always been a big issue in our country, and it continues to be so in our culture. The Bible speaks of freedom as well, of men made free—the truth sets free and the Son sets free.

Free from what?

I. The Domination of Death

A. Life's greatest enemy—death

B. Mankind lives in fear of death

C. The resurrection of Christ has set us free from the fear of death

II. The Supremacy of Sin

A. Sin tends toward dominion

B. Freedom in Christ breaks the power of sin

C. The child of God can never say that he can't help sinning—all sin is optional

III. The Grind of Guilt

A. Guilt can be worse than the punishment for its cause

B. Guilt can actually be a punishment

C. The children of God need never feel guilt for longer than the time it takes to dawn on them that they are feeling that way

IV. The Curse of Care

A. You can call it by whatever name you wish—worry (weight of worry)

B. It comes from many sources in various ways and takes a great toll

C. He has set us free from care

D. Like sin and guilt, any care we carry is purely optional on our part

V. The Pressure of People

A. People wear on us in various ways—we even become fearful of them

B. There is no need to sense pressure from people—do what is right in the sight of the Lord and all will be well

C. He sets us free from all forms of the "fear of man."

VI. The Fear of the Future

A. Our eternal future is secure

B. Our temporal future is also in His care

C. He has set us free from bondage to the uncertainties of life—there is no need to dwell on the future

VII. The Slavery of Self

A. We develop little ways of getting our own way

B. These ways carry into adulthood—what once held others captive now holds us in bondage (pouting, temper, silence, bullying, etc.)

C. He has made us free from bondage to ourselves

Conclusion:

Can we celebrate our own freedom? What holds you in bondage? What will you do about it?

Doing God's Work

John 9:4–5

Introduction:

God's work! It's being a pastor, an assistant pastor, or a missionary. Or teaching Sunday school, ushering, working with teens, singing in the choir, driving a Sunday school bus. Both definitions are just part of the picture. It's more basic; there's more to it than just that.

I. We Are to Do God's Work

- A. Translation
  1. "I" should be "we" (NIV has it right)
  2. "WE must do the work of HIM who sent ME"
- B. There is a demand in it—"must"
  1. An intense word of requirement
  2. We are all required to do God's work
- C. We are to work in place of anything else
  1. The disciples wanted to speculate
  2. He would have no part of it—He put the focus on work

II. The Work of God That We Are to Do

- A. The things that He did
  1. Relieved suffering
  2. Rebuked wrong
  3. Taught truth
  4. Encouraged the troubled
  5. Touched lives
  6. Won the lost
- B. The spirit that characterized His work
  1. He did the Father's will—"Him that sent me"
  2. He was a servant of servants
  3. He was unable to bypass a need
- C. The pattern it presents us
  1. This work is bigger than, prior to "God's work"
  2. This work is required of each of us
- D. The challenge He leaves
  1. "While I am in the world, I am the light of the world"
  2. "When I am no longer in the world, ye are the light of the world"

III. The Urgency of God's Work

A. It must be done while there is time
   1. A familiar proverb—"the night cometh when no man can work" (v. 4)—people in that day were unable to work at night
   2. We must work *now*

B. Note the "must"—your involvement is not optional
   1. This work gains us no standing
   2. This work wins us no special favor

C. Make no mistake—it is work!
   1. The things in view here are harder than "God's work"
   2. This is demanding because it draws on what we really are

Conclusion:

God's work is more than the ministry or church work. God's work is doing—to the extent that we are able—the work that God sent Christ to do.

"I Belong to the King"

John 10:22–30

Introduction:

A composer said:

I belong to the king, and He loves me I know,
For His mercy and kindness so free,
Are unceasingly mine, wheresoever I go,
And my refuge unfailing is He.

Our relationship to Him is personal, intimate, individual, private, and particular.

I. You Can Belong to Him

- A. Notice His wording
  1. "My sheep"
  2. "My Father . . . gave them to me" (KJV)
- B. Notice His distinctions
  1. "Ye are not of my sheep"
  2. You don't have what my sheep have
- C. Note the facts
  1. Only some people belong to Him
  2. Those people do belong to Him, and you can be one who does

II. What It Is Like to Belong to Him

- A. When you belong to Him, you have the assurance of His presence
  1. Hear His voice (v. 27)—discern it, delight in it, do it
  2. Be assured He knows you (v. 27)—He singles you out of the mass of humanity
- B. When you belong to Him, you have a sense of purpose
  1. He goes before (v. 27)
  2. "Christians not only obey Christ, but they imitate Him; they go where His Spirit and providence lead them; they yield themselves to His guidance and seek to be led by Him"
- C. When you belong to Him, you have certainty regarding the future
  1. "I give unto them eternal life" (v. 28)
  2. Relief from perishing (v. 28)—"Perishing is a terrible fate and to be delivered from it is a priceless gift. Salvation is from real peril, real disaster, real tragedy"

D. When you belong to Him, you have complete security
   1. Two statements:
      a. No one will pluck you out of His hand (v. 28)
      b. No one is able to pluck them out of my Father's hand (v. 29)
   2. Intense meaning here—our security rests on His hold on us, not our hold on Him
E. When you belong to Him, you become part of something special
   1. Retranslate verse 29: "that which my father gave me is greater . . ."
   2. His people—the church—are incredibly important, not because of who they are but because of what God has done in them

III. How You Can Get to Belong to Him

A. It is not a matter of information
   1. They question who He is (v. 24)
   2. They had plenty of information (v. 25)
B. It is not a matter of evidence
   1. The works He had done should have sufficed
   2. They had failed to be convinced (v. 25)
C. It is simply a matter of belief (v. 26)
   1. They were not His sheep because they wouldn't believe in Him
   2. We become His simply by believing in Him

Conclusion:

I belong to the King, and it is a marvelous relationship. I became His by believing in Him. Do you belong to the King? You can if you will.

The Problem with Peter

John 13:2–20

Introduction:

You can almost always find Peter before the crucifixion. He is usually the "man with his foot in his mouth." The incident at the footwashing may reveal many of the reasons he was such.

Notice Peter's problems, which came on two levels.

I. **Peter's Incidental Problems**
   A. He was proud
      1. He remonstrates with Christ, but he made no effort to replace Him in the task
      2. He wanted to be a spectator, not a recipient
   B. He was stubborn
      1. "Never"—not now or in the foreseeable future
      2. This may have been his weakness that caused the reaction
   C. He was impetuous
      1. "Not my feet only, but also my hands and my head" (KJV)
      2. If a little is good, a lot would be much better

II. **Peter's Major Problems**
   A. He did not want to accept the implications of Christ's actions
      1. Peter didn't understand all the details, but knew what was going on
      2. He simply didn't want to face what was indicated
      3. This is behind much "inability to understand" Scripture
         a. It is not that we don't understand what it says
         b. It is that we don't want to do what it says
   B. Peter did not want to accept what he could not fully understand
      1. There were details that had escaped Him
      2. He didn't see how things fit together, therefore he couldn't accept this
      3. There is much "crisis of faith" even among Christians—we accept what we can see working out, but we reject what we can't understand

C. Peter did not want to accept things that were other than the way he thought they should be
   1. He had his own ideas on how things should be done; Christ did not act in accord with his ideas
   2. He did not want to accept the fact that Christ might have other ways
   3. We struggle with the same thing—we have our idea of how things ought to be done, and we don't like it when Christ does otherwise

D. Peter did not want to come to terms with the lordship of Christ
   1. Christ had a right to do as He wished; Peter had no reason or excuse to question His ways
   2. He had not come to accept lordship
   3. We have trouble with His lordship—we struggle because we won't accept biblically unchangeable situations as being part of His will for us

Conclusion:

The biggest problem with Peter is that he is so much like us. We don't want to accept the implications of God's actions. We don't want to accept what we can't understand. We don't want to accept things done in ways other than as we think they should be done. But our basic problem is accepting the lordship of Christ.

Doing so means seeking His help to change what can be changed, seeking His help to live triumphantly with what can't be changed.

Cooperate in the Pruning

John 15:1–8

Introduction:

Let's look at a necessity for productivity in the Christian life—pruning. God wants us to be productive. This passage tells us the price.

I. The Process of Pruning

Most of us already know too much about this

- A. God uses people to prune us
  1. This involves all the ugly things people do to us and say about us
  2. These are often people who themselves have not developed the fruit of the Spirit that we are working on developing
- B. God uses problems to prune us
  1. The problems that we bring on ourselves
  2. The problems that come upon us outside our control—we are dealing here with the circumstances of life
- C. God uses pressures to prune us
  1. This has to do with the ways in which we respond to problems
  2. There is a sense in which all pressure is self-created

II. The Purpose of Pruning

- A. Pruning is positive
  1. God has purposes for everything He allows to come our way
  2. Nothing comes by accident or "happenstance"
  3. "Surely your wrath against men brings you praise"
- B. Pruning is powerful
  1. God always achieves His purposes in this world
  2. We are given the option of cooperation
  3. The more we accept His working, the more it accomplishes, and the more quickly it is over
- C. Pruning is productive
  1. The fruit of pruning is first internal (Heb. 12:11)
  2. Pruning is necessary in producing the fruit of the Spirit
  3. Pruning contributes to the productivity of our lives and ministries
  4. Notice the progression in John 15—fruit, more fruit, much fruit

III. The Problems of Pruning—Mistakes Regarding Pruning

A. Pruning is punishment
   1. It is clear from Hebrews 12:4–11 that this is not so
   2. Our punishment was taken by Him on the cross
   3. Chastening is simply part the pruning process (the dead branches)

B. Pruning is permanent
   1. We think the branches will never grow again, the loss permanent
   2. Pruning is done so that more fruit will be produced
   3. There is an end to pruning or the plant is destroyed, which is never God's intention

C. Pruning is passive
   1. God prunes out the dead branches
   2. God also prunes the living branches (He sometimes cuts back something we consider very productive)
   3. Our refusal to accept what He is doing can cause us to miss productivity

Conclusion:

God wants us productive. God is always at work in our lives to produce the fruit He wishes. Maximum productivity demands that we cooperate with His pruning.

Getting a Conviction

John 15:1–16

Introduction:

A question about your convictions:

If Christianity were illegal, would there be enough evidence to convict you?

The underlying question: How does anyone know you are a Christian?

I. The Usual Answers to the Question

A. I practice personal separation

B. I make verbal expressions—frequently talk about Christianity

C. I have charismatic signs

II. The Biblical Answers to the Question—Analogy of Fruit

A. The fruit of the Spirit (Gal. 5:22–23): "fruit" is singular

B. The fruit of good works (Eph. 2:10): the purpose of salvation

C. The fruit of souls won (John 15:16): the idea of winning people to Christ/Christianity

III. The Key to the Answer to the Question—John 15:7

A. Abide in Him

1. Continue, endure, dwell, remain
2. Find your ultimate source, rest, satisfaction, etc., in Him

B. Let His Word abide in you

1. It takes up residence
2. It becomes the dominant factor in life

C. Communicate with Him

1. Prayer is part of abiding in Him
2. We overlook the fact that fruit is borne as a result of abiding in Him, His word abiding in us, and prayer

IV. The Significance of Your Answer

A. There is a danger in not bearing fruit—this is shown in John 15:2–6

B. God's other work—everyone experiences problems (including Christians, and there are two groups of Christians: those whose problems are to prune them, and those whose problems are to purge them)

C. The danger of not bearing fruit is to experience God's purging

Conclusion:

If Christianity were a crime, would there be enough evidence to convict you? How does anyone know you are a Christian? If it were only by fruit-bearing, would they know? Why are you not bearing fruit? Wouldn't it be wonderful to know that trials, etc., were the result of God's pruning rather than His purging?

"Unless I See . . ."

John 20:24–29

Introduction:

In those days, twins were often a surprise, and they'd give the chosen name to the first; sometimes the second was merely called "the twin," and that appears to have been so with Thomas.

Maybe it accounts for his generally negative, doubting personality type. He really outdoes himself following the resurrection of Christ.

I. Thomas Was a Robust Doubter

A. He had been negative to begin with—he had suggested death with Lazarus

B. There was no way he was going to accept the Resurrection

C. He demanded physical evidence, which he never expected to see

D. Doubt grows by what it feeds upon

II. Thomas Was an Honest Skeptic

A. He expressed his doubt openly—note his questions about heaven, etc.

B. There was never any question of where he stood

C. His words are negative but exactly what he felt

D. Honest doubt is better than fake faith

III. Thomas Was an Astonished Witness

A. Christ appeared in the room

B. He invited Thomas to do what he had claimed he would require

C. There is no record Thomas took Him up on the invitation

D. Christ's presence made a touch unnecessary

IV. Thomas Was a Confirmed Convert

A. His encounter with Christ answered his questions and solved his problems

B. He makes an amazing statement that goes beyond Peter's expression

C. The change here is dynamic and dramatic—it comes from seeing Christ

D. "Jesus, you are my Master and you are divine [God]"

V. Thomas Was a Typical Disciple

A. We tend to look down on him because of his sensory demand
B. Actually all the other disciples were the same
C. Others, unnamed, were more praiseworthy
D. To this point, everyone had seen, then believed

VI. Thomas Is a Challenging Figure

A. He shows us the deepest unbelief (he had been with Christ, seen His miracles, etc.)
B. He shows us the greatest conversion
C. He shows us the way—belief in Christ
D. Belief provides the greatest evidence

Conclusion:

Thomas said, "Come on, get real!"
Jesus said, "I am real; see for yourself."
You say, "Come on, I can't see:
That this is real;
How this is going to work;
Why something like this should make a difference;
What difference this can possibly make."

In most of life, to see is to believe. In the spiritual life, to believe is to see.